D1257962

Pär Lagerkvist

by

LEIF SJÖBERG

 **Columbia University Press**

NEW YORK 1976

COLUMBIA ESSAYS ON MODERN WRITERS
is a series of critical studies of English, Continental, and other writers
whose works are of contemporary artistic and intellectual significance.

Editor
George Stade

Advisory Editors
Jacques Barzun   W. T. H. Jackson   Joseph A. Mazzeo

Pär Lagerkvist is Number 74 of the series

LEIF SJÖBERG
is Professor of Comparative Literature and Scandinavian Studies
at the State University of New York at Stony Brook.
He is the co-translator, with W. H. Auden, of
Selected Poems: Gunnar Ekelöf and *Evening Land: Aftonland,*
by Pär Lagerkvist.

Acknowledgment is made to Wayne State University Press for
permission to quote from *Evening Land: Aftonland,* by Pär
Lagerkvist, translated by W. H. Auden and Leif Sjöberg, English
translation copyright © 1975 by Wayne State University Press; to
Random House, Inc., for permission to quote from *The Sibyl,* by
Pär Lagerkvist, translated by Naomi Walford, copyright © 1958 by
Chatto and Windus, Ltd., reprinted by permission of Random
House, Inc., and from *The Death of Ahasuerus,* by Pär Lagerkvist,
copyright © 1962 by Chatto and Windus, Ltd., reprinted by permission
of Random House, Inc.

15 5655

Library of Congress Cataloging in Publication Data

Sjöberg, Leif.
  Pär Lagerkvist.

  (Columbia essays on modern writers; no. 74)
Bibliography : p.
1. Lagerkvist, Pär Fabian, 1891–1974—Criticism and
interpretation.   I. Series.
PT9875.L2Z85   839.7′8′7209   76-9052
ISBN 0-231-03103-3

Columbia University Press
New York   Guildford, Surrey
Copyright © 1976 Columbia University Press
Printed in the United States of America

Pär Lagerkvist

In a small, modern country like Sweden writers tend to become public persons, somewhat in the sense that actors and actresses do. This is not peculiar to Swedish authors only; indeed it is a striking phenomenon in all the Scandinavian countries, particularly in Iceland, where there is greater per capita interest in local authors and their books than anywhere else in the world. Accordingly Scandinavian authors are expected to grant interviews to the press, appear on radio and TV, present public readings, take part in panel discussions, serve on committees and prize juries, and autograph their books at book fairs.

Pär Lagerkvist, however, was a major exception to this code of behavior and politely declined such public exposure. In December, 1940, when he was elected to the Swedish Academy, his acceptance speech, a summation of his predecessor's achievements, turned out to be his first public address. Lagerkvist was then forty-nine years old and had published more than twenty-five books. When in 1951 he received the Nobel Prize for literature, he could not avoid an international press conference but he was brief in his comments. When asked questions about his personal life and tastes, he simply referred reporters to his books—in them he had expressed all he wanted to say. As a young man, however, Lagerkvist had had a very different attitude toward the writer who isolated himself, as Erik Hörnström and Sven Linnér have found out; this is a point which we shall return to later.

Pär Lagerkvist was born in 1891 in Växjö, Småland prov-

[3]

ince, in southern Sweden. He was the last of seven children born to a railroad employee and his wife. It is important to point out, however, that his parents had moved from the country to the city only a few years earlier and that they kept up their contact with their country home to the extent that, while living in the city, they were more country folks than city dwellers. Their attitudes were, by and large, traditional; their religion, especially that of Lagerkvist's grandparents, almost identical with the old peasant religion—dominated by the Old Testament and larded with various bits of Pietism. They were generally suspicious of new ideas. They had no interest in international politics and little in national or local politics. If and when they voted, it was for conservative candidates. To establish an analogy here the reader might consult Vilhelm Moberg's *The Emigrants* (tr. 1949), which depicts Småland peasants emigrating to Minnesota and New Sweden. In Pär Lagerkvist's home also the Bible was apparently read aloud daily, chapter by chapter, until it was finished, and then it was time to start all over from the beginning.

It is typical that Lagerkvist's father, who had become a signalman *(bandgårdsförman)* in Växjö, refused to join the railroadmen's trade union, even at the risk of losing a chance for a better salary. "God in this world wishes to maintain order and difference between people," wrote Arndt in his book of family sermons which was read in the Lagerkvist home. "[He] Himself has arranged the classes and without them the world cannot endure. The earthly advancement each of us ought to receive, God will let us experience in due time without our doing. If He should let us stay in the lowly position where we stand, that is also according to His will, and we shall console ourselves with His grace and with the hope of eternal life."

Such teachings, pleading for the *status quo* as they did,

went unheeded by Pär Lagerkvist. At school he learned about Darwin's theory of evolution, in which terms like "struggle" and "natural selection" played such great roles, and opened up entirely new possibilities that his parents did not understand but that he himself wanted to explore. And he did!

Lagerkvist thus experienced the break between the epochs of the old farming society and the industrial revolution (which reached Sweden more than a century later than in the United States and Great Britain). Of necessity this experience also entailed a break with his parent's religion. He has described this break in *Guest of Reality* (*Gäst hos verkligheten,* 1925), a title that could be taken as an allusion to Arndt, "that in this world we do not have any continuing city," i.e., we are guests of reality. But since almost everything in Lagerkvist's writing is ambiguous, we can also read the title as a parallel to Eyvind Johnson's *1914* (London, 1970): "He knew that his life would not be like theirs. He was certain of it. . . ." He was only a guest.

Lagerkvist had decided while still a boy that he wanted to become a writer. At school he kept very much to himself and tended to be an outsider. He was a better than average pupil but apparently antagonized some of his teachers so that his grades varied from "A" to "F" in Swedish composition. On occasion he went so far as to challenge sharply his teachers' criteria for marking.

The petit bourgeois environment at Växjö was intolerant of any deviation from the *status quo.* Lagerkvist and four of his classmates rebelled against this inflexibility and formed an organization they called "The Red Ring." They held "anarchist meetings" on Sundays, at 11 A.M., at the very hour when the cathedral bells were calling the people to service. Their radicalism was largely apolitical and theoretical and above all was concerned with religion. Among books dis-

[5]

cussed were those by the immensely popular astronomer Camille Flammarion, the embryologist Thomas Huxley, and Kropotkin (*Memoirs of a Revolutionary* and *The Struggle for Bread*), as well as various anarchist and socialist tracts. From Scandinavian authors they read, for example, Ibsen's *Brand* and Strindberg's *Master Olof*, both concerned with Christian revolutionaries. But above all Darwin's *Origin of Species* was of fundamental importance to these young revolutionaries since, as years later Pär Lagerkvist stated, it shook "the very foundation of the transcendental view of the world." And it emphasized life as a process of change alternating between growth and decay.

During his last few years at school Pär Lagerkvist contributed to several newspapers. Beginning with a conservative one, he moved on to a liberal one and by 1909 had been radicalized to the extent that he began to write poems and political songs for two socialist magazines.

He studied the history of art at Uppsala, 1911–12, but was soon disillusioned by his studies at the university. Instead he published his first book, *Människor* (*Human Beings*, 1912), a talented debut, although one critic ridiculed him by claiming that the book consisted of about 1,200 words and about 12,000 dashes. It should be noted that the year 1912 has since been termed a watershed in Swedish literature; it was the year in which Strindberg died and Lagerkvist's debut occurred.

It was only in 1913, however, that Lagerkvist made his real impact on the Swedish literary scene with his *Ordkonst och bildkonst* (*Word Art and Pictorial Art*), subtitled "About the Decadence of Modern Fiction, About the Vitality of Modern Art," which has many ideas in common with Denis's manifesto "Définition du Neotraditionisme," 1890. This 60-page pamphlet opened with a barrage against contemporary Swedish literature, which was judged cheap and commercialized, lacking in serious artistic ambition, putting too much emphasis on abnormal psychology. In it Lagerkvist energetically stresses that it is "the poet's task artistically to elucidate the [present] time for us and future generations and to give artistic expression to its thought and feeling." He goes so far as to state that in a certain sense "there exists no modern *belles lettres*, a literature that mirrors modern man's idea of life, his way of thinking, seeing and feeling." The documentary approach has been taken over by popular science and is, therefore, no longer needed; further, the writer as polyhistor is an old-fashioned ideal that passed with Strindberg. Consequently the study of reality will have to be approached by other methods.

What remedy did Lagerkvist see for literature? He had visited Paris for about a month in 1913 where he had seen and admired Cézanne, Gauguin, Matisse, and the Cubists and had associated with radical artists. He had found the "decadence" in literature startling when compared with the flourishing situation in the fine arts. With approval he quotes from Apollinaire's *Les peintres cubistes* (which he had reviewed earlier in the year) and generally places his hopes on Cubism. Art should attempt to become *pure* and be based on mathematical principles. Cubism had an appeal to Lagerkvist as both "anti-naturalistic" and "rational"; furthermore, it *constructed* its results the way modern architects and engineers did.

"Conscious and consistent simplicity in the psychological realization—that is no doubt one of the main conditions for a more elevated art culture: simple lines, that might aim at the stylized, decorative, monumental; simple characters in the presence of whom one is forced to take an interest in them less because of what is human than for the concentrated, strictly *unified* power in their composition and the strangely balanced proportions they display of themselves."

[7]

Supported by quotations from Poe's brilliant aesthetic essays, Spencer's extraordinary "The Philosophy of Style," Robert Louis Stevenson's "Essays in the Art of Writing," Lagerkvist argues in line with the Cubists that "real beauty" rests on mathematical concepts, independent of time. Apart from Cubism one can learn from Flaubert, Baudelaire, and others, but above all from ancient and primitive cultures. Pär Lagerkvist calls for a Gauguin of literature.

Contemporary fiction has to rely on a number of sources for renewal—the *Kalevala*, the Finnish folk epos, and Icelandic literature, "an inexhaustible treasury." He remarks on the "immense concentration" of "Völuspá," and the simplicity in style and structure in Old Norse sagas. Other sources of renewal might be the poetry of ancient Egypt (*The Book of the Dead* [2500 B.C.], *The Book of the Breath of Life*), Assyro-Babylonian literature ("myths, tales, prayers, incantations, dirges cannot help but affect us"), and, above all, Indian literature ("encountering it is like going from admiration of human feats of strength into ecstasy at the wonders of the human spirit"). He singles out the Vedic literature, the *Rigveda*, Kalidasa's, dramas, and the Pali canon as particularly outstanding; in them he finds perfect artistic, formal, and imaginative unity. He does not fail to mention the Bible, the Avesta, and the Koran.

In summing up; Lagerkvist regrets that contemporary Swedish fiction has come so "hopelessly far away from seeking the ineffable and the sublime." However, by penetrating into modern art's theoretical and ancient poetry's practical knowledge about means and goals, the creative writer should come to an understanding of what direction to take. Contemporary writers would have to learn a new "artistic observation, artistic shaping, and artistic seriousness." Lagerkvist's program displays considerable erudition for a twenty-two-year-old author. In Sweden, it is generally regarded—in retrospect—as revolutionary, an eye-opener of great importance and, for Lagerkvist in particular, as a revelation of his literary ideal—*simplicity*. In his words, an author should employ "simple thoughts, uncomplicated feelings in the face of life's eternal powers, sorrow and joy, reverence, love and hatred, expressions of the universal which rises above individuality." For years Lagerkvist stuck to the rule of simplicity.

While Lagerkvist was indeed a true believer in Cubism and other new art, energetically speaking out for them during 1913–16, he gradually modified his views and dropped the term "Cubism." One thing that he repeatedly stressed in these early articles is that art should be an expression of contemporary time's own basic character. Considering that Lagerkvist was, largely, contributing to socialist papers, he took a decidedly deviant view in favor of *l'art pour l'art* and against *Tendenz:* he saw art as "reality itself, only in other forms; the proportions are magnified, the material is refined but the very inner expressive power is the same; it is the same blood but other limbs, a new and noble *Gestalt.*" Referring to the unproductivity of art during the French Revolution, Lagerkvist implies that art is independent of social upheavals and asserts that although socialism may choose one direction, art has its own way to go.

Pär Lagerkvist had been writing one-act dramas since 1911, although in his first polemical pamphlet he had virtually ignored drama. When reviewing a production of Hofmannsthal's *Everyman* performed at the Swedish Royal Dramatic Theatre in 1916, Lagerkvist complained of "the new strong feeling for style *(stilkänsla)* which, in modern pictorial art, has failed to any measurable extent to inspire the art of the stage." He was critical of both Max Reinhardt and (mistakenly) Gordon Craig, the most innovative directors of the time. Lagerkvist, who many times before and after revealed his interest in medieval art and drama, its forms and symbols, suggested that *Everyman* should have been acted with greater audacity and "in a formal, grave, severely stylized manner," not with individual mannerisms nor hovering between simplicity and realism. A preliminary version of *Teater*, 1918 (published in English by the University of Nebraska Press, 1966), is partly an outright attack on naturalism, which according to Pär Lagerkvist still dominated the stage through World War I in spite of the fact that it was unable effectively to express "the violent and abrupt contracts in modern life . . . all that is complex, confused and fantastic in the situation." He saw our time as "much more fantastic than Naturalism is able to portray. In our daily lives we scarcely possess the feeling of security that the form of naturalism still implants, we hardly have it when facing reality, but rather an ardent need of finding expression for all that anguish with which life now [during World War I] fills us."

His target was Henrik Ibsen. Lagerkvist claimed that perfection in evil as well as good is reached in a typical Ibsen drama "with silent pacing of the carpets throughout five long acts of words, words, words. . . . Perhaps one could venture the statement that Ibsen is great for the sake of his merits, not for his faults, not because through his authority he has happened to work for the limitation of modern drama to a rather limited area?"

Lagerkvist's ideals were medieval drama on the one hand, and Shakespeare and the later Strindberg (i.e., those plays after *Inferno*, such as *Advent*, *To Damascus*, and the *Chamber Plays*), on the other. He pleaded for a new use of theatricality independent of naturalism. The new playwright, like Strindberg in the *Chamber Plays*, should aim at releasing one single mood, one single feeling, and not attempt to analyze man psychologically nor draw his "character"; he should only give "images of man as he is when evil, when he is good, when he has sorrow, when he experiences joy." And Lagerkvist quotes with approval from Yeats's foreword to *Plays for an Irish Theatre,* defending poetic drama. What Lagerkvist asks for is "a new Romanticism? A more variable, more violent and more ecstatic form? A more abrupt and simpler view?" But it is not a return to neo-Romanticism he wants to achieve, not flight from reality; clearly he wants to explore a deeper level of reality, seeing "the fantastic elements in things themselves and in reality itself." A new form, according to Lagerkvist, created out of inner necessity would be the prerequisite for a real Renaissance.

Ångest (*Anguish,* 1916), a collection of expressionistic poems showing strong organization and with anguish as the main theme, opens:

> Anguish, anguish is my inheritance
> the wounds of my throat
> the screams of my heart in the world.

In *Anguish* we also find a poem titled "Salvation Army":

> A moment ago a human being found God.
> How the room radiates clarity.
> A little being in grey
> worn clothes which wrap
> their shabby shell about her body,
> about her warm and slender limbs.
> With trembling hands she gropes
> about in the blue and lofty spaces,
> and climbs on burning feet
> up and up towards the floating stars.
> (*excerpt:* tr. with W. H. Auden)

It appears as if Pär Lagerkvist was ambivalent even about the theory of evolution, as is evident from this anti-Darwinist prose piece from *Anguish:*

[11]

"It irritates me, the thought of all these lower, more or less abortive, animal forms which have preceded man in the uncertain development upwards; it never deserts me! If I go in a gorgeous car through the big brilliant city in the evening, when everything is a veritable sea of light, in which the houses become chalky white, the streets shiny as a mirror and people elegantly fantastic, I nonetheless think I hear the animals howl out of the forests in the deserted land and all kinds of vermin crawl forth on the ground. It is excruciating. The ecstasy I wanted to be seized by when facing man—it always suddenly is disturbed by the thought of the ridiculous in his family tree."

The writings in *Anguish* had been influenced by the brutality of World War I, and for the first time Lagerkvist ironically proclaims the death of God.

> About me lies eternity
> about me you o God, are silent.
> What is big and empty like eternity,
> what is silent, reticent like you, o God."
> (literal translation)

In that desperate book as in many subsequent works Lagerkvist tends to oscillate between extremes, yoking together a need for loneliness and fellowship, a hankering for life and an obsession with death.

With his theoretical underpinnings stated in *Teater,* what were some of the practical results in Lagerkvist's own playwriting? His first published play, *Den sista människan (The Last Man,* 1917), depicts an earth that is a frozen wasteland. The sun is gradually cooling. Everything is fading away. The last humans rove about, dwarfed, on the dying land. In this apocalyptic passion drama, the crumbled remainders of a cityscape loom "like the limbs of lepers." Man has returned to the cave, from which muted voices are heard. A scream comes *out of the earth:* Anguish! Anguish! (relating the play to German Expressionist *Schreidrama*). A leprous man states the problem: "There is no love anymore in the world! Only hatred . . .!" Among the crawling humans, competition is still fierce for the last rotting slices of meat. Gama, the central character, introduces himself as in a medieval morality play: "I am the Blind Man! The great blind man! I lie down here in the darkness! I have been lying here for a thousand years! No, for ten thousand years I have been lying here!"

Gama is "the last man." He has groped around the area about himself, but never found what he was searching for. "I have not lived! Do you hear? I cannot die! I cannot," he exclaims. He is a confused, Angst-ridden being, who has violated love by rejecting the love of Vyr, a woman who, in revenge, has put out his eyes. Between the two is Ilya, the innocent boy, a symbol of love. Later, Gama strangles Vyr when he finds out who it was who had blinded him. Ilya dies, before Gama. If this reminds us of a Strindbergian marriage scene *(Dance of Death)*, it is also the kind of "absurd" tragedy Lagerkvist wanted to write.

In *The Last Man*, as in several of his other dramas, questions centering on death, and on good and evil, are the main themes. The grotesque and the fantastic dominate. Unlike the naturalist drama, which he attacked in *Teater*, Lagerkvist abruptly introduces all kinds of nightmarish qualities, anguish, and psychological peculiarities. While Ibsen and Strindberg (after *Inferno*) present individuals in tragic personal conflict, Lagerkvist attempts to tackle universal problems among humans in their final, loveless misery.

Lagerkvist's *The Secret of Heaven* (*Himlens hemlighet*, in *Kaos* [*Chaos*], 1919) was produced privately in 1919 and 1921 (among the cast was a young actress who was to become the immortal Greta Garbo). As he often did, Lagerkvist uses a cosmic perspective. The setting of the play is the upper part of a bluish-black sphere, indicating the earth, on which an old man is sawing wood. "He never raises his head, does not look around, tends only to his own affairs," a symbol of *deus absconditus*, the unconcerned god, whose presence is also felt elsewhere, for example, in *Guest of Reality*. Also in the cast are an old man, a man on crutches, a dwarf, a hangman who decapitates dolls, a girl, and a boy. In this hopeless world, the boy falls in love with the girl who, however, responds negatively. The desperate boy cries, full of anguish: "Save me! Save me!" and asks the old man about the meaning of life. He gets the answer that everything will keep spinning 'round and 'round. The boy throws himself out into the darkness to perish, accompanied only by the indifferent laughter and chatter of the last few decrepit representatives of man. This is, literally, "stop the world I want to get off." (The staging was effective; in fact, Gordon Craig had used a similar approach in Ibsen's *The Warriers of Helgeland* in 1903.)

The Eternal Smile (*Det eviga leendet*, 1920) pursues the same question as *Chaos*, i.e., the meaning of life, but the questions are now raised by, allegedly, the dead ones, "the greater majority," who sit in groups here and there in the great darkness chatting together "to make eternity pass." Each is relating something from his or her life on earth. Some of their stories are bizarre, or dreamlike, or everyday descriptions, but others are short stories in themselves.

In this "kingdom of death" the inhabitants think longingly of their lives on earth. Most of them are the *simple*, ordinary kinds of characters Pär Lagerkvist clearly loves to delineate. One is a caretaker of an underground public lavatory, "an ordinary man," who did a job for an "ordinary man," and he became happy. Another, a shy workman, is longing for home.

He tells of his home and his little son who used to come and sit on his lap and play with him until he fell asleep in the evening. Family life had been his salvation. He cannot forget the lilt of his wife's voice. He remembers the pattern of the plates, a picture on the wall, the chest of drawers, and the old brown sofa. Somewhere else, a twelve-year-old boy and a girl sit talking, constantly, of little, poetic experiences they had had in the countryside. Then there is the moving story of the locksmith who has forever locked himself out of love, of a merchant who doubted that there was any life after death and who was surprised that "there was one after all!" There are a man and a woman who are in love, a headwaiter, a murderer, and others who only listen: a man who has lost his wife in childbirth and who has been killed in an earthquake (one of the Italian elements of *The Eternal Smile,* written after Pär Lagerkvist's first visit to Italy in 1919).

There is also the grandiose story of the young man who, toward the end of his earthly life, one evening lost his way and halted at a mill. The miller's fat wife locked out the miller and offered the delicacies of the house, herself included, to the young man, who turned out to have a Gargantuan appetite. Guilt feelings took over and, in ecstasy, he finally met his end in the grinding millstones, while the miller exulted (like the Icelandic smith Völund).

If most of the characters are "ordinary" there are also some extraordinary ones, among them the three "saviors" who speak up. Each calls himself "the savior of man." The first one, clearly Christ, claims his life was "announcing suffering and death to man, saving them from the joy of life." He had called God his Father and Heaven his home. He was crucified. After the darkness of Golgotha men knelt around his cross and "hated me, their Savior." He had trusted in his mission and his Father but, "When I came here I had no father. I *was a man like you*," he says, "disillusioned." "And life's sorrow was not my sorrow. Life's sorrow was a happy sorrow, not the one I carried."

A fanatic who is a philosopher commits the first revolutionary act among the dead by standing up and voicing Pilate's question: "What is truth?" He cannot endure his "loneliness in a space without end. . . . We cannot be saved, we are too much. We find no road that we all can wander." Life is full of confusion. Can life never be *simple,* unified? he asks and decides to "seek God, that is always truthful." Now everybody suddenly realizes "what helpless confusion life meant, that it was so much and so great that it gave none of them any peace, not even to the happy one." They realize that they have to orient themselves toward "something else, to something which applied to them all, to clarity and certainty, to truth." While some say there was no god for them, the zealot explains that "one single man could not expect to have a god; but for us millions there has to be one." Then they believe him.

The fanatic thus leads the myriads toward god. And now they experience fellowship; their feeling of loneliness disappears and they find "meaning" in existence. There is no confusion, no anguish, no loneliness: "no one was so strange that there was not a few millions like him." They feel no need to seek god any more. They comprehend everything themselves, there is hardly anything to comprehend. "Things only are the way they are. . . . Life seems only to mean that they should exist and that they should go well together. It is a meaning so simple that there is nothing to say about it, nothing."

However, another revolutionary, a philosopher of a different persuasion, declares that he hates this life of endless repetition. He claims he has lost that which he had felt as the holiest within him. ("No confusion, no sorrow, no misery, no bleeding wound. No quivering heart that never will find peace. Nothing! Everything that to us meant life's riches and pain, which filled us with anxiety and searching disquiet, with a longing without boundary, that is nothing.") That is why he wants to seek God in order to demand the return of "confusion and doubt, the soul's longing which can be quieted by nothing, to demand from his unboundedness, his anguish, his space without end."

Then the multitudes start off again. They wander through centuries and millennia while thinking of God ... They never arrive. Finally, after more centuries of wandering they see a light, a light throwing its beams over *an old man cutting wood.* They can see that it is God. He is so busy sawing that he does not notice them. People ask him what he has meant to do with them. Humbly he admits that he had meant nothing in particular. He has only done "as best as I could." The answer does not satisfy the people; especially the elite among them are disturbed by it. The old man says, "I am a simple man." Quietly he reveals that he has worked without requesting anything for himself, neither joy nor sorrow, neither faith nor doubt, nothing. "I have only meant that you should never have to content yourselves with nothing." Then the elite are quiet, but the ordinary people bring forward their children and ask: "What did you mean with these innocent little ones?" "I meant nothing by them," the old man says quietly. "Then I was only happy." They all deeply and mysteriously feel their intimate fellowship with God. They *"understand that he is like themselves only deeper and more"* (italics added). Having experienced the good in the world which the title of the book may refer to (Hörnström), the masses are satisfied and return, filled with trust and gratitude. An old man says, "I recognize you, dear life, as the only conceivable among all that is inconceivable." Another says: "It is man's duty to be happy." "All the riches in them which their thoughts could not fathom, they secretly hid within themselves, when parting, to return each to find his place and to go on living."

At the very beginning of *The Eternal Smile* Lagerkvist specifies that a few dead ones "sat talking in the darkness. They did not know where—perhaps no where," and later, he says twice: *"to be dead, i.e., to belong to eternity"* (italics added). Here Lagerkvist discounted the Christian division between heaven and hell. The idea becomes clearer if we note that Christ appears in this realm of the dead, with "everybody else" so to speak, holy men as well as murderers. By showing Christ and other saviors of man as men of wishful thinking, mistaken in their beliefs that they had a mission to save mankind, and by showing God as a mere woodcutter, Lagerkvist accepts the idea that both God and His Son are as simple as "one of us." Here, as in the story "The Morning," it is vaguely implied that God is created by man, a reversal of the Bible's version of man as being created in the image of God. God, here, resembles any father who wards off his children's impertinent questions by humbly avowing that he has done the best he could. In *The Eternal Smile,* Lagerkvist plays down the transcendental aspects in favor of life on earth: eternity is "perhaps nowhere," so man had better stake his hope on his life in *this world:* the fear of death in general, so characteristic of Lagerkvist's early writings, seems to have been checked, if not completely conquered.

In the short story "Father and I" (*Evil Tales,* 1924) Lagerkvist tells of a walk in the forest he, as a ten-year-old boy, took with his father. When dusk falls the boy is frightened by the fears he conjures up. He sees darkness everywhere and does not dare breathe deeply for fear he will swallow too much darkness and therefore will have to die. He asks his father why it is so eerie when it is dark, and gets the answer that it is not eerie. "After all we know that there is a God."

They are strolling along the railroad and are menaced by the sudden appearance of an unscheduled train, a ghost train. They barely save their lives by jumping down the embankment. "What sort of train was it? There wasn't one due now! We gazed at it in terror. The fire blazed in the huge engine as they shoveled in coal; sparks whirled out into the night. It was terrible." The engineer "stared straight ahead," as though intent on rushing further into the darkness.

The blazing locomotive engine, a kind of epiphany, is seen by the boy as a symbol of his—perhaps also of modern man's—future life:

"I shivered in my whole body. It was for me, for my sake. I divined what it meant, it was the anguish which was to come, all the unknown, what father did not know anything of, against which he could not protect me. Such this world, this life was to become for me, not like that of my father's, where everything was secure and safe. It was no real world, no real life. It only dashed, blazing, into the darkness that had no end."

Guest of Reality (*Gäst hos verkligheten,* 1925) is of interest as one of the rare autobiographical narratives by Pär Lagerkvist and as an illustration of how in practical terms Lagerkvist applied his own program: he uses a narrative technique with a simple, concrete style ("artificial simplicity" as one reviewer said) close to spoken language, and concentrates on *one* recurrent theme in order to achieve an effective wholeness. That theme is the obsessive concern with death and the process of dying of Anders, the main character.

Anders is the youngest member of a signalman's large

family, which occupies two rooms and a kitchen on the second floor of the station house. *Outside* is a variety of change that children observe from the narrow windows: railroad cars switched about to form new trains or onto new tracks, passengers waiting for trains at the railroad restaurant, occasional military transports, or the regimental orchestra playing.

Outside, "there was never any calm, always people in a hurry to leave." *Inside,* in the home, there was a portrait of Martin Luther above the bureau, old and new Bibles, Arndt's collection of homilies, floors covered with homewoven carpets in many colors that deadened one's footsteps. "It was almost always quiet in there, although they were many."

Anders is clearly an unusual child. He is introspective and hypersensitive, with early fears of death that soon become obsessive and develop into certain compulsive actions, such as his visiting the ice-cellar or, on oppressive, rainy days, his praying on a flat stone in the forest for the lives of everyone. Anyone who, like this boy, finds life so feverish will also experience the fear of what he hates most: obliteration. Thus the boy's fear of death can be seen as connected with an intensive lust for life: his youthful temperamental outbursts are signs of disharmony, but when he appears preoccupied with death, he is actually appalled by it rather than attracted to it.

The obsessive fear of death in the child is nonetheless abnormally pronounced. In a superstitious environment which relies solely on fundamentalist religion for guidance, and with a grandfather who says, "It is good to hear thunder, then one is reminded that God is in power," sin is likely to be a byword—while death, of course, remains the punishment for sinning. However, assuming that severe guilt feelings in children develop primarily in puberty, the death-fear in Anders would perhaps have been more convincing had it developed at a somewhat later stage in his life. But then a need for naturalism would probably have made for an entirely different novel. The boy rebels against the oppressive mood at home. "All that kindness, all that affection there was at home—you couldn't bear it. Never a raw gust of wind to sweep in . . . And his parents' fear of God, heavy and time-honored, an ancient peace which they attempted to experience—while sighing, only sighing. It pressed down, as if it wanted to suffocate you. . . . You had to break out of it." The alternative to the parents' beliefs is the "new" doctrine, i.e., Darwinism, that Anders has picked up, "which swept God away and all hope, which laid life open and raw in all its nakedness, all its systematic meaninglessness; that was better; that helped. And it was true, too. *No faith—just things as they are*" (italics added). He wishes to become free. But the degree of his liberation is seen in the final episode of the book where he attends a prayer meeting at the Salvation Army. He observes everything from the outside, unable to become excited or ecstatic. ("He stood outside, as it were. Like someone listening by a door.") But the young Salvation Army officer for whom he waits after the meeting (and who praises God) reminds us of his own mother. He is attracted to the idea of being saved by such a woman, yet he is also compelled to reject it firmly.

"They walked quietly for a long while. . . . He stood watching—as if he was in love with her? . . . So ended his early youth, in nothing but dissolution, falsity, confusion." Anders is both attracted to and repelled by a mother-figure.

If anxiety is a state in which received impressions fail to form a meaningful pattern, Anders is in such a state.

The novella *Bödeln* (*The Hangman*, 1933) opens with a scene in a murky medieval taverna where, by himself, the awe-inspiring hangman (executioner) in his blood-red attire drinks his beer. Journeymen and apprentices look with fear and curiosity at the hangman. Old artisans talk about him both as a sinner and as someone who is to be pitied. In their vulgar way they speculate on the strange, magic healing power which the Hangman's sword or other tools of evil can possess.

They note that a murderer's blood has cured an epileptic boy and that children suffering from rickets have been cured if given blood scraped off the hangman's sword. "Yes, it is obvious that the hangman must have a power like no one else, as close to evil as he is. And that his broad-axe and all such things have healing power in themselves, that is for sure," says one artisan. Another (who sounds like Pär Lagerkvist) says: "Evil is not easy to get to know fully, and if one does, it can happen that one is filled with wonder." He then proceeds to tell the story of how, as a child, he had done that forbidden thing and had actually played with the hangman's children. He had even touched the broad-axe, an act which, according to beliefs, destined him later to die by that axe. But the hangman had showed "mercy" and had removed the curse from the boy by thrice, according to ritual, letting him drink water out of the hangman's hand. It was as if a wonder had happened! One hangman is said to have been smitten by love on the place of execution and to have saved his victim by marrying her, but eventually he became her hangman: when her child was born with the hangman's mark, she murdered it and, by society's own cruel self-imposed laws, the hangman was forced to bury her—alive! (Pär Lagerkvist has taken pains to stimulate his reader's sympathy for the hangman.)

By stating that the tragedy ended with the disappearance of this medieval hangman, Lagerkvist announces, by implication, the appearance of the modern hangman. It is only that we fail to recognize him: he has become so indistinguishable from ourselves. Yet he is in our midst! There is no longer any need for the office of the hangman/executioner: each of us has accepted this role for himself and is willing to conduct his own executions.

While the hangman, immovable, silently looks out in the darkness, by some magic the scene is transposed into a dance hall of the early 1930s. In the play version the transition is highly effective. "Having witnessed the medieval scene with all its horror, it is a shock to see that all this suddenly becomes a pure childish idyl when we encounter our own time" (Malmström, 118). On his way to Palestine in 1933, Lagerkvist had passed through Berlin and therefore knew what was his target and why. At the time of publication, *The Hangman* was felt clearly to be directed against Nazism and Fascism, but a sophisticated reader will not fail to note that the message is actually more universal and is also directed against all violence and racism.

While in Part One the hangman is presented to the medieval artisans as an executioner and/or scapegoat, in the *modern* scene he is presented as a distorted ideal. In the modern environment, violence is considered the highest expression of man's physical and spiritual powers: "War is healthy"; "War is the sign of nobility on a man's forehead." In Part Two, the hangman is the epitome of what the patrons of the night club consider the greatest in life.

When the hangman finally speaks, it is in an overlong, obscure speech in which he reveals that he resents being man's scapegoat and that at the time, when he had crucified God's Son, he had protested to God. But God had been immovable or unmoved: he did not claim any responsibility for Christ. "He belonged to mankind, and it was (therefore) not strange that he had been treated in the way they treat their own kind. It was only one of their own kind they had crucified, as usual," concludes the hangman. Just as the

[23]

drunken modern-day soldier is disappointed in the hangman for not knowing his job properly ("Why doesn't he use a machine gun? . . . You should be in uniform, old chap!"), the hangman once was disappointed in Jesus and thus missed his chance of being saved. ("No. He was no savior. How could he be? He had hands like a half-grown youth. . . . I wondered if they were strong enough to hold him up there? How could a man like that possibly be the redeemer of mankind?") Then the hangman realizes why *he* has to serve man, saving by war or destruction rather than by peace. While man has caused God to petrify and die long ago, the *idea* of God, the *principle* of God, and the duality of good and evil have survived and are still effective forces, especially the fitter of the two, namely evil. This powerful *idea,* God, had begotten *with* mankind "while he was still omnipotent and alive and knew what he wanted!" The hangman is sure *he* will not be crucified. If he is the principle of evil of all times, he will so remain to the end of time. He is part and parcel with man's tragic evolution.

But totalitarian modern men have desensitized themselves to the extent that they know neither guilt nor atonement. Human evil is exactly as eternal as man. In spite of a mysterious forgiving love, man's feeling of guilt is such that he imagines even after his work is done he will "still be hunted like a restless phantom through the darkness of the heavens, the length and breadth of my father's great tomb, persecuted by my tormented love and haunted by the memory of what I have done for you!" He longs for his sacrificial death. Has Lagerkvist been too negative, too pessimistic? He was aware of what was going on in the world at that time; his force in shocking his audience can be seen as a great humanistic endeavor, requiring considerable courage. A positive note at the end of the book is perhaps the fact that a loving woman will be waiting for the executioner when his work is done:

the horror of the modern world has not driven out the possibility of redemption through love.

In Lagerkvist's *The Dwarf* (*Dvärgen*, 1944), a chronicle allegedly written by a dwarf called Piccolino, a hangman appears only in the final pages, "big and ruddy-faced and naked to the waist," thus unlike the central character in *The Hangman* and with a somewhat different function. The hangman of this novel of the Renaissance is supposed to torture Piccolino so that he will reveal his mistress's illicit relationships. But the dwarf (who is no more than 26 inches long) does not measure up to the size of human implements of torture. When finally tortured, he endures the test like "heroic" men, imitating them by not revealing any secrets. There are reasons for this: in his peculiar way he relates to people of power and action like the Machiavellian Prince Don Riccardo, Boccarossa the Condottiere, and Fiametta, the Prince's mistress, but is totally unable to relate to the others, especially Bernardo/Leonardo and Angelica, whom he hates because he does not understand them. In general he hates people ("is there anything as disgusting as men") for the games they always play and for not being like *he* is. Piccolino's own love life differs sharply from that of the Princess: while she always has loved many, he has loved no one (except himself). If there is anyone he could relate to it is the Princess.

When after scourging her Piccolino says to her, "May the flames of hell forever lick your loathsome lap, which has enjoyed the terrible sin of love," his outburst is characterized by the excitement that generally accompanies sex. He himself acts as her potential abortive lover. While being her *postillon d'amour* he has observed her voluptuous way of living for years.

While he protects her secrets even under torture, it is

worth noticing that he has received them in "confession," and thus under the seal of secrecy. She calls him "God's scourge," which he accepts with some hesitation. If he is "God's scourge," his "dual nature" has at least demonstrated how good and evil can be intertwined and related; he is the unloving, selfish instrument of evil, but he is also part of the whole—life in its dualism. (His crime: that he wants to be the whole.) When, guilt-ridden, she finally dies she has been transformed. Led by the Prince, people genuflect and pray at her simple coffin. The candles burning in her memory draw the attention of everyone who walks into the church because there are so many. Rumors of the mortification of the Princess circulate and the myth of her sanctity is then *being created*.

The dwarf is deeply surprised that "a man of so little holiness" as himself could be used for something like this. It is, in fact, he who has created her halo "or at least contributed to its luster," he ironically remarks: but the one who above all, unintentionally, contributes to the iconography built around the "saint" is Bernardo/Leonardo, the artist inventor.

He was himself not much of a believer (in God's mother) yet, with his painting (a mysteriously smiling "Mona Lisa"), he creates profound religious feelings in people attending church. Thus the dwarf somehow indirectly causes others to rise above their baser instincts, in the long run releasing powers which lead toward "higher" realities. All aspects of life, once again, are shown as intertwined. Certainly Bernardo (a giant in the world of the spirit) provides the church with the sanctified image of the Princess as the transformed one, as the saint, but he also leaves behind a picture of her as a whore. The latter picture is hung in the castle (incidentally, close to and protecting the church) and not seen by those who have the need to see saints. This "double view" of men,

[26]

including Bernardo, is something Piccolino does not have, nor does he comprehend it. He is in fact closer to the Princess than he is to his master, the Prince. The dwarf comes into contact with the whole range of religious paraphernalia from the Madonna (or the making of one) to the Holy Communion. He himself was baptized at a mock ceremony when he was eighteen and he vigorously counts himself as a Christian, but he is a most hard-headed conventional bigot who, like so many men, believes in the Christian dogma only for as much as he can make use of it. In different ways he is associated with the Last Supper, to Christians a central rite as *agape*, or the sacrificial meal with Christ's presence felt. In a real sense the dwarf witnesses the Last Supper in Santa Croce "with the celestial Christ sitting among His disciples at their love feast with Judas the betrayer crouched in his far corner," as it is *envisioned and portrayed* by the most creative giant of the Renaissance, Bernardo/Leonardo. Yet as can be expected, the dwarf remains unmoved by the experience.

In spite of a great deal of brooding over what religion is, the dwarf is none the wiser; he admits he remains unenlightened. It does not help him to an understanding of the rite, not even when he is so close to the mystery or the sacrifice as to be the *officiating functionary* at the Last Supper. He knows the Christian formulas, but can only pervert them into blasphemy.

I raised the crucifix and all the dwarfs fell on their knees. . . . "Here is your savior," I declared in a sonorous voice, my eyes flaming with passion. "Here is the savior of all the dwarfs, himself a dwarf, who suffered under the great prince Pontius Pilate, and was nailed to his little toy cross for the joy and ease of all men." I took the chalice and held it up to them. "This is his dwarf's blood, in which all inequities are cleansed and all dirty souls become as white as snow." Then I took the Host and showed it to them and ate and drank of both in their sight as is the custom, while I expounded the holy mysteries. "I eat his body which was deformed like yours. It tastes as bitter as gall, for it is full of hatred. May you all eat of it. I drink his blood, and it burns like a fire which cannot be quenched. It is as though I drink my own.

"Savior of all the dwarfs, may thy fire consume the whole world!"

And I threw the wine out over those who sat there, staring in gloom and amazement at our somber communion feast. . . . I am no blasphemer. It was they who blasphemed, not I. . . .

What was meant as merely a parody becomes real enough, not only for the officiator: the Prince and especially the Princess and his guests are frightened. "They think that I am the one who frightens them but it is the dwarf within them, the ape-faced manlike being which sticks up its head from the depth of their souls." It is after "that last supper incident" that Theodora, the Princess, goes through her transformation.

When the dwarf was asked to "officiate" at the Machiavellian Prince's gala banquet to celebrate "eternal peace," he identified with his role fully, according to his nature, in the most negative, destructive sense.

"I felt like Satan himself, surrounded by all the infernal spirits," he says, and "nearly lost consciousness" from joy at his temporal power. At the Last Supper as commemoration of his death, the dwarf administers the wine (with the poison) of the rite to make it, literally, into the last supper—of his enemies. But it is significant that the dwarf fails to "redeem" young innocent Romeo/Giovanni. Certainly he is killed later, but only after having experienced that which the dwarf is incapable of attaining—*love*. There are many things the dwarf also fails to comprehend: among them, human conscience, the grace of God, salvation, or the Gospel.

It has been suggested (by Oberholzer) that *The Dwarf* is the best constructed and most multifaceted novel Lagerkvist has written. In the text there are allusions not only to Nietzsche but also to Hitler's *Mein Kampf* and, naturally, to Lagerkvist's own previous creations. Some little echoes are not insignificant: God is indeed dead: "the Crucified One answers nothing" (p. 138). Giovanni's mother "is *said* to be in paradise"; when the campanile will be completed, the bells will "resound *like up in heaven*" (p. 12); when the bells finally resound, Anselmo talks of "the indescribable sound which *seemed to* them to come from Heaven" (italics added). "Mankind does not like to be raped by God" (p. 33).

Barabbas (1950; dramatized version, 1952) became Lagerkvist's most successful novel, which, after winning considerable international success, assuaged the Swedish Academy's objections to awarding the Nobel Prize to a native Swede.

The book contains more religious paraphernalia than any other work by Pär Lagerkvist up to that date. "There are so many gods one cannot keep track of them all," says the Governor in one passage. Some of them are mentioned, but they are unimportant in comparison with God's Son, who in many ways dominates Barabbas. According to Matthew, Barabbas was a notorious convict, who Mark and Luke say was imprisoned on charges of rioting and murder. John calls him a robber. Hjalmar Söderberg, Lagerkvist's fellow-countryman, had tried to make it probable that Jesus and Barabbas were the same person, since Barabbas in some manuscripts had the same first name as Christ. Renan saw Barabbas as an insurgent and killer. Mauriac in his *Life of Jesus* made Barabbas a robber, as did Lagerkvist. In the very beginning of his book Lagerkvist makes Barabbas an eyewitness at Golgotha. This point is of fundamental importance, since Barabbas here is for the first time given the opportunity to become a witness for Christ. The action is largely the same as in the four gospels, but seen through the eyes of Barabbas, the robber. "The story, therefore, appears as a fragment of a fifth, parodic gospel, where the crucifixion of Jesus is only an episode of no consequence in the everyday life of Jerusalem" (Nils Norman). In his fantasy Lagerkvist has taken the historical facts lightly and has introduced viewpoints that belong to modern times. He reminds the reader that modern man is perhaps himself a Barabbas. By keeping a few biblical quotations intact and by using certain other devices Lagerkvist manages to maintain a level of verisimilitude. Lagerkvist constantly shifts his technique in relating the characters to each other.

The sturdy robber does not care for Jesus and is unimpressed with a man whose body is lean and spindly, lacks hair, and is clearly weak. One thing amazes Barabbas nonetheless: how such a wretched man can have "such a strange power" to command him to attend the crucifixion, especially since he is superstitious about Golgotha. "Actually he had not wanted to go up here at all, for everything was unclean, full of contagion. . . . If only the end would come! . . . As soon as it was over he would rush off from here and never give this another thought!"

In those passages Barabbas's future is outlined. Without in any way realizing it, he is drawn to his own destruction, by crucifixion.

The thought he intends to shut out of his mind, i.e., Christ's ignominious death on the cross, is the very thought with which he will be obsessed throughout his life, even at his own crucifixion. Barabbas's situation is unique. Being a robber and manslayer, according to the prevailing law he should surely be put to death (Leviticus, 24:17). But Christ promises the robber on the cross, "Today shalt thou be with me in paradise." Christ is more in favor of sinners than righteous people (Mark 2:17); so that what Barabbas considers his own deficiency actually makes him eligible for salvation: he only has to believe and to realize that he is sinful. Here there is no theological casuistry or wishful thinking that Christ has died for mankind: Barabbas is physically on hand when Jesus Christ, literally, dies in *his* place.

But the mind of Barabbas works the other way. He is convinced that Jesus was innocent and was amazed that the high priests could judge him as they did. Barabbas had seen Jesus surrounded by an inexplicable dazzling light in the courtyard of Pilate's palace but later attributes this light to a trick of vision after having suddenly been taken out of a dark prison cell.

When *darkness* (a main symbol) falls on Golgotha, Barabbas, like the others, is frightened. When the solar eclipse is over, "everything at first is as usual. It only had become dark for a while because he died." This expression is a stylistic and religious understatement (N. Norman) of the same kind as in Strindberg's *A Dream Play* where Christ, in a storm scene, comes to save shipwrecked people: "He is just one who walks on the water."

Barabbas's ambivalence to Jesus as the Son of God is amply illustrated in *Barabbas*. While Barabbas is drawn to the poor quarters of the first, simple-minded Christians, he also despises them.

He has "come," as Barabbas's woman, the Harelip, says— and she may refer to Christ or Barabbas—but neither has the power to stop the stoning. Barabbas shows his power by stabbing to death the man who threw the first stone at her. Barabbas tries to display his power but actually reveals only his impotence. He offers another display of violence when he returns to the robbers' hideout in the mountains. What is on his mind he reveals in action when, without apparent motivation, he stabs various members of a caravan carrying tithes to the High Priest, while remaining inactive when the band murders a Roman sentinel. Barabbas's aggressiveness is directed against those high priests who inexplicably released him rather than Jesus, and not against the Romans

[31]

in whose jail he became "the one almost executed." (This idea perhaps reflects the near execution found in Stig Dagerman's *Den dödsdömde,* which had appeared a year earlier.)

Barabbas's initiative and authority in the band are now gone and soon he disappears. However, the memory of how he became their leader after killing Eliahu remains. With all the rebellious "outsiders" in Lagerkvist's work, it is not surprising here to find one father-murderer (Lagerkvist's only one), and no psychological sneak-murder but an outright fight for superiority, which in Lagerkvist's view has its counterpart in Christ's sacrificing *his* life at the alleged call of *his* Father. Of Barabbas's fate when he reappears twenty years later, Lagerkvist remarks that some think he devoted himself to brooding over God's and man's world, others that he had joined a sect that hated priests and scribes. Thus it is hinted that Barabbas was still bothered by his release in place of Jesus.

Barabbas is now a slave, and as a slave he is in deep need of a merciful master. Joined, literally, with a Christian, a true believer called Sahak, Barabbas asks him to inscribe on his own slave's body the sign of the fish, Ichthys, which word transliterated from the Greek forms an acronym indicating that he belongs to Jesus Christ, God's Son, Savior of man.

Sahak, who feels saved by the crucifixion of Jesus, is himself crucified for not renouncing his belief, while Barabbas looks on with the sign of the fish crossed out (!) on his slave's badge: it is a symbol of divided belief, abortive belief. Released for the second time in conjunction with a crucifixion, Barabbas is sent to Rome where, again, he is drawn to the early Christians. Among the dead in the catacombs, where they hold their meetings, Barabbas experiences loneliness in existential terms, "alone in heaven and on the earth, and among the living and the dead."

On his return, the eternal city is afire. Barabbas gets a false sense of witnessing the final destruction of the world and the resurrection of Christ as an avenger. Now he has the message: he throws one fire brand after another until he is seized.

In the end he is crucified as a "Christian." The taciturn Barabbas utters the ambiguous words, "To thee I deliver up my soul," when he felt death was approaching. André Gide took this to mean that Barabbas died a believer. But the ambiguity in the last sentence should be related to Lagerkvist's own religious views. If consistency in views can be assumed, Lagerkvist, in *The Clenched Fist* (*Den knutna näven*, 1934), made a clear, strong statement: "I am a believer without belief, a believing atheist." When hiking in Galilee, Lagerkvist says he was thinking of Jesus and the mysteries surrounding the character of Jesus: "I wonder who you were, you who wandered here on the roads—the same as now. I do not know; nor does anyone else either. You belong to myth and the legends." Here Lagerkvist appears to be an agnostic and Jesus is in his stated opinion not God.

In *Aftonland* (1953; *Evening Land*, 1975, tr. W. H. Auden and Leif Sjöberg), Lagerkvist's ninth and final volume of poetry, his main theme is again man's relationship with a god, "a god who may not even exist." Since *Evening Land* is the only collection of Lagerkvist's poetry available in English, a few observations about it will have to suffice. Lagerkvist explores the religious question from many points of view, and they all seem to originate in a mysterious religious experience in childhood:

> Who walked past the window of my childhood
> and breathed on it?
> Who walked past in the deep night of childhood,
> that still was starless?

With his finger he made a sign on the pane,
on the moist pane
with the ball of his finger,
and then passed on to think of other things,
leaving me
deserted for ever.

How should I be able to interpret the sign,
the sign in the moist afterwards of his breath?
It stayed there a while, but not long enough
for me to be able to interpret it.
For ever and ever would not have sufficed to interpret it.

When I got up in the morning, the window-pane was
    entirely clear,
and I only saw the world such as it is.
Everything in it seemed so strange to me,
and, behind the pane, my soul was filled with loneliness and
    longing.

A cosmic-religious experience in the past is thus postulated, but the child "only saw the world such as it is," i.e., without the aid of a faith.

But Lagerkvist keeps exploring different religious sentiments:

Let my shadow disappear into yours.
Let me lose myself
under the tall trees,
that themselves lose their crown in the twilight,
surrendering themselves to the sky and the night.

It should perhaps be noted that "shadow" in the biblical Orient is something good: protection against the blazing sun (cf. Psalm 91). While the poet seems trusting, believing, and perhaps willing to surrender or to be abandoned in God ("let me lose myself"), in the next poem his relationship as a child to his father is indicated.

Hold me in your unknown hand,
and do not let go of me.

> Carry me over morning-bright bridges,
> and over the dizzy depths
> where you keep darkness imprisoned.
>
> But darkness can no longer be imprisoned.
> Soon it will be evening over your bridges,
> then night.
> And perhaps I shall be very lonely.

In almost existentialist terms it is stated that with or without a merciful father there will (perhaps) be loneliness and darkness; with that insight, death and uncertainty is the one certain thing.

In the final poem of this group, the outsider, the individualist and rebel, never far away in Lagerkvist, perceives man's *fight* against anxiety, loneliness, alienation, death wishes, suffering, and despair as something in itself positive and meaningful, perhaps because it compels man to attempt to transcend himself, in dreams, imagination, religion, creative work:

> May my heart's disquiet never vanish.
> May I never be at peace.
> May my path be unending, with death its unknowable goal.

To be sure, the poem is a prayer to someone, but at the same time it is a declaration of independence, even of a certain defiance. The three poems above exemplify the wide range of attitudes in *Evening Land.*

A desert wanderer, again an outsider, appears in these poems in different disguises: man alive, death, and sometimes as a god or gods. In the childhood memory eternalized in a poem such as "With old eyes I look back" the wanderer is obviously the poet-narrator:

> My soul has been chosen to search far away
> for hidden things, to wander under stars.

But the theme of the wanderer in the same poem is intertwined with that of the stranger:

> What did I experience that evening,
> that evening in Fall when I went to fetch wood for mother?
> I remember it so well, I remember no other evening like it.
> It was then that for the first time I saw the stars.
>
> With the billets of wood in my arms I came to look up into
>   the sky,
> and then I saw them there, surrounded by a boundless
>   darkness.
> Everywhere above me they existed in a desolation without
>   end.
>
> I stood there absolutely still. And everything vanished for
>   me,
> everything which had been there before, everything which
>   had been mine,
> my little horse with three legs, my rubber-ball,
> my joy at waking up in the morning,
> the sunshine, the stone-marbles and the big glass-marble,
> all my toys.
>
> When I got back to mother again and set down the logs by
>   the kitchen range,
> certainly there was no noticeable change in me, certainly
>   not.
> But when I went and sat down on my footstool far away from
>   the others,
> I was no longer a child.

It is symbolic that when he has come indoors, he sat down
on his footstool "far away from the others," like someone
who does not belong, or someone who must be apart from
the others. To the one who considers himself "chosen," and
assumes that there was once made a mysterious sign "on his
childhood window," everything in the world suddenly
"seemed so strange" (pp. 100–101). Barabbas, and the Sibyl
and Ahasuerus (whom we will meet) in Lagerkvist's novels
are such "chosen" ones, outsiders, loners, doubters; and so
are a number of "saviors" (in *The Eternal Smile*, "Savior

John," the hero in "A Hero's Death" in *Evil Tales*, and the hero in the play *The Invisible One*) and those who identify with a negative savior such as the dwarf, or the medieval man's scapegoat, the hangman. It can be argued that Anders in *Guest of Reality* is chosen to see "the world such as it is," and yet to have an eternal longing.

The "stranger" in the poem opening *Aftonland*, IV, according to Kai Henmark, may be "the god whom Pär Lagerkvist will fear the longest, namely death":

> I should like to be someone else
> but I don't know who.
> A stranger stands with his back to me, his forehead
> facing the burning home of the stars.
> I shall never meet his eyes,
> never see his features.
>
> I should like to be someone else
> a stranger, other than myself.

To Anders, the main character in Lagerkvist's *Guest of Reality*, God and death are intertwined concepts. On the one hand, death, or the fear of death, can bring man closer to God. On the other hand, one of God's attributes, such as thunder, can cause death and destruction through lightning. ("It's good hearing it thunder, then you know for sure that God is in power," said the grandfather in *Guest of Reality*.)

"Under the influence of the stranger-childhood god, the poet transforms himself into a stranger, and becomes an equal to god. Literally in the name of god he can talk of the feeling of loss, when the young bird leaves its nest—god and man are easily mistaken for the other, filled with longing, yet impartial" (Henmark):

> I am the hand from which the fledgeling flew,
> the hand of the creator.
> It will never return to me,
> to its nest.
> Nothing returns to me.

In the poem above, Lagerkvist thus uses the persona of god, and it is worth noticing that *god* appears *lonely* or disappointed at his creation, just as in another poem describing the land of death *man* feels abandoned and *lonely:*

> They all have fled, all my friends,
> the summer wind, the dewy grass in the morning,
> the fragrance in the forest after rain. I am all alone.
>
> All the fountains of life
> have fallen silent.
> Abandoned, abandoned.

In a group of poems Lagerkvist puts forth an idea, which may remind us of Ludwig Feuerbach, that reverses the process of creation: we humans invented god, not the other way around:

> It is not god who loves us, it is we who love him,
> who reach out for him in longing after something else,
> someone greater than ourselves

But paradoxically:

> If you believe in god and there is no god
> then your belief is an even greater wonder.
> Then it is really something inconceivably great.

As Henmark has pointed out, faith and substitutes for faith, such as religious symbols or trappings, tend to substitute for god as the focus of devotion in Lagerkvist's work. Judging from the poem about the spear-caster, it is Lagerkvist's contention that the force of that faith (represented by the spear-caster) originates nowhere except within man himself. However, in an apparent ironic twist against himself, Lagerkvist in the final stanza asks: "why is that not enough for you?" i.e., acceptance of a god as something necessary and entirely human, even in the most extraordinary times.

The Sibyl (*Sibyllan,* 1956) deals with a former pythia, or high priestess, at Delphi who, while serving Apollo, literally experiences his presence, in ecstasy, as his sexual love-partner. As her fame as a pythia grows, she recognizes that she remains an outsider, different from others. In an attempt to change her status to "insider," so to speak, she embraces a stranger, a man (later killed by the river god) by whom she has a son. He turns out to be retarded, with a fixed, meaningless smile on his face. While the Sibyl tells her story to a visiting stranger, actually the Wandering Jew, Ahasuerus, her son vanishes from the top of Mount Parnassus—evidently he has ascended to heaven. If so, the Sibyl has to admit, she has borne the son of the god rather than of her sometime lover in the valley. Thus her relation to god is again suddenly and drastically changed.

As when she for the first time had served as pythia and expected to gain peace and happiness, she learns otherwise:

I felt relief, release; a feeling not of death but of life, life—an indescribable feeling of delight, but so violent, so unprecedented. . . . It was he! He! It was he who filled me, I felt it, I knew it! He was filling me, he was annihilating me and filling me utterly with himself, with his happiness, his joy, his rapture. Ah, it was wonderful to feel his spirit, his inspiration coming upon me—to be his, his alone, to be possessed by god. By his ecstasy, his happiness, by the wild joy that was in god. Is there anything more wonderful than sharing god's delight in being alive.

God, the mysterious one, is different. When ecstasy has passed, the Sibyl feels an even greater loneliness than before. "God could not be as I wished him to be, as I so much wanted him to be. He could not. God was not security and repose and rest. He was unrest, conflict and uncertainty. These things were god."

In fact, she tells Ahasuerus of a double aspect of god: He is constantly "within me, fills me with his presence, with his unrest, that never gives me peace, because he himself is not peace." She sums up her experience of the divine by saying that "the divine is not human." And she continues: "And it is not noble and sublime and spiritualized as one would like to believe. It is alien and repulsive and sometimes it is madness. It is evil and dangerous and fatal . . ." As far as she can make out, god is "both evil and good, both light and dark, both meaningless and full of meaning which we cannot perceive." To this pythia, god appears to be everything that she is unable to comprehend: miracle, mystery, ecstasy, dreams, and her irrational acts. If there are obvious biblical paralells with the Sibyl's god, they are not infrequently of a negative, even mocking, kind.

As the one ostracized from fellowship with men, Ahasuerus, another outsider, is familiar with unrest, the turmoil of his own soul, and he can, therefore, relate to the Sibyl's analysis of "god's dual character" (Henmark). The curse of Christ he hears over and over in his mind, but without knowing by whom it is repeated: "By myself? I don't know." To him the sign of god's existence is precisely the eternal unrest in his own soul. And he says (on the final pages of the book) that he will always roam around, "driven by the unrest that he [god] fills me with, without ever finding peace."

However, god manifests himself even in other ways, i.e., as some of Lagerkvist's poems suggest (like "The Spear-Caster"), as man's own creation. Especially Kai Henmark and Andreas Skartveit have emphasized that this alternative is to be found in Lagerkvist. Man "creates god, breathes him out of his unrest and equips him sometimes with the best and sometimes with the most terrible thing within man" (Henmark). Lagerkvist had hinted at this idea already in a Narkissos-like prose sketch, "Gudstanken" ("The Idea of God," 1912), and in the short story "Morgonen" ("The Morning," 1920). Lagerkvist's essentially "homocentric" view of religion as man's own response to various needs is clearly formulated in this story (contrasting life in Sweden and Italy), ending thus: "And above us reigns men's God, *our mysterious creation*" (italics added). A similar idea was expressed among American humanists in the 1880s and 1890s. It has been maintained that in Lagerkvist's latest books, god "does not become a person in the sense of drama. . . . He becomes an image of man, i.e., created by man—and the story of creation is reversed" (Skartveit). This is, of course, a considerable overstatement of the case. Lagerkvist is, as so often, ambiguous. If the homocentric view were to exclude nonhuman concepts and images of god, the loss would be disastrous both in *The Sibyl* and in Lagerkvist's work in general.

Many characters in Lagerkvist, outsiders like Barabbas, the Sibyl, and Ahasuerus, have been part of god's reality, i.e., they have met god. While their experience has had a profound effect on them, to the extent that everything is colored by the meeting, they feel they have been, largely, "victimized" rather than "saved" through god's visitation. The same holds true in *The Death of Ahasuerus* (*Ahasverus död*, 1960), which differs technically from *Barabbas* and *The Sibyl* in that Lagerkvist gives only glimpses of individuals and environments, in an impressionistic manner. But the interminable monologues continue, as before. The book consists of two parts: the first, a *Rahmenerzählung* about the encounter of Ahasuerus and the "false" pilgrim Tobias and the Artemis-like Diana; the second, the great monologue of Ahasuerus. The latter, although brief, is the essential message of the book, and begins with a question addressed to god that is reminiscent of questions raised before by Lagerkvist: "Why do you persecute me? Why do you never leave me in peace. Why do you never abandon me?"

Ahasuerus has, indeed, reason to speculate about why *he* of all those who fail to recognize god should be singled out for unjust punishment. Ahasuerus, however, develops: he recognizes Christ as his brother, and this, as Henmark has stressed, breaks the ego-isolation of Ahasuerus. Obviously it also refers to his religious concerns.

The latter part of Ahasuerus's monologue opens with an echo of what Tobias has told him:

There must be something which for man is of the very greatest importance. That I have learned. Something which is so important that it is better to lose one's life than to lose one's faith in it.

Beyond the gods, beyond all that falsifies and coarsens the world of holiness, beyond all lies and distortions, all twisted, divinities and all the abortions of human imagination, there must be something stupendous, which is inaccessible to us. Which, by our very failure to capture it, demonstrates how inaccessible it is. Beyond all the sacred clutter the holy thing itself must exist. That I believe, of that I am certain.

God is what divides us from the divine. Hinders us from drinking at the spring itself. To god I do not kneel—no, and I never will. But I would gladly lie down at the spring to drink from it.

That credo is often taken as Lagerkvist's own, especially since it has been stated earlier in different versions, for example, in *Kämpande ande* (*Struggling Spirit*, 1930).

The *Rahmenerzählung* (inset story) in which Ahasuerus is transformed and liberated, at last to die, is open to varying interpretation because of the use of symbols such as the sea, the locket, in spite of its simplicity on the surface. A key-word is "peace." But, as always, Lagerkvist's work defies simplistic, definitive interpretations. Tobias, the main character in the story-within-a-story, is himself without a center and becomes a pilgrim *by chance*. But in the process he encounters his fellow-beings and recognizes their need of love, an achievement as good as many a pilgrimage.

[42]

Pilgrim at Sea (*Pilgrim på havet,* 1962) and *The Holy Land* (*Det heliga landet,* 1964) are, by and large, the continuation of Tobias's pilgrimage on board a pirate ship with the defrocked priest, Giovanni, to whose bizarre love story Tobias will listen. In *The Holy Land* the fates of Giovanni and Tobias become ever more intertwined; Giovanni even saves the life of Tobias, in a literal sense, and through "the sacrament of conversation," an art of confession (it is really for all practical purposes a monologue), as Skartveit has observed, the parties are "transformed into fellow-beings to each other."

Scenes and characters in *The Holy Land* are more rhapsodic and closer to the surrealistic than in any other Lagerkvist book. Giovanni, who has lost his faith and blasphemes, and the bandit Tobias, who involuntarily became a pilgrim, have landed on a strange rocky coast that suggests a land other than the Holy Land, but not far from that of traditional religion. They make their home in a ruined temple, dig up a *deus absconditus*, still with a scornful smile on his lips, and discover that a Christ-cult has developed among the shepherds of the region. When their sheep begin to die en masse, they resort to magic to stop the disease from spreading and ask an augur for advice. Tobias notes, to his dismay, that these innocent, good-natured shepherds who watch the herds of sheep do not belong to human beings but to the sheep themselves; that they actually enjoy inflicting pain on sacrificial animals. Does Lagerkvist here hint that men of all ages are alike and can endure their own misery better when observing the vicarious suffering of other beings, whether crucified or, in the case of animals, when used for divining purposes (as the Romans said: *haruspicina*)?

In the last chapters, when Tobias is left alone after the death of Giovanni, the well-known scene with the triple crucifixion is seen in stark relief against the sky. It is significant that Tobias is attracted to the cross of the innocent one at the same time that he is repelled by it: "It is nothing for me. I do not dare touch it with my blood-stained hand, not this cross." He feels related to the two robbers on the left and the right side of Christ and *can* touch "the bandit's cross. *My* cross."

Also in the final scene, an obscure dream sequence, the outsider Tobias encounters a person literally closest to Jesus Christ, i.e., his mother, Mary. Through her he achieves what even Giovanni has reached through the intermediation of a woman: peace of mind. The two outsiders, Giovanni and Tobias, through their deaths join "the greater majority," and these two rebels achieve atonement and peace. However multilayered and ambiguous the trilogy may prove to be, the end is partly unconvincing and without great imaginative force. The hazy dream wandering through various *stations* is too obscure for a logical interpretation.

In his final novel (and the only one that is a love-story), *Mariamne* (1967), Lagerkvist deals in passing with Herod's child murders in conjunction with the birth of Christ. The three wise men who appear toward the end are not holy kings, nor do they present the newborn child with gold, incense, and myrrh. Instead they offer a small stone, abrased at the sea shore, a thistle in the shape of a spire which has grown in the desert sand, and a small jar of water, also fetched from the desert. To those familiar with Lagerkvist's usage of these symbols in early works the novel takes on dimensions and significance which are perhaps equally apparent otherwise. And there are other references to Lagerkvist's early work, as well. Herod differs from such characters as the outsiders Barabbas, the Sibyl, Ahasuerus, Giovanni, and Tobias in that he is obsessed with the problem of unrequited love, rather than with divine love. Instead of philosophizing he acts out his neurosis in wars, violence, and rape, and since he constantly sets himself as the center, he has in fact "no connection with the divine." As Lagercrantz has suggested, Herod is an anguished hero. When he builds a temple to a god in whom he does not believe, when he forces his love on Mariamne who cannot return it, he contradicts himself, he is in conflict, but he nonetheless resembles man of modern times more than the above-mentioned characters. He turns out to be "an image of man."

Mariamne belongs to the many bright, good lady characters in Lagerkvist's portrait gallery, perhaps the coolest and least approachable of them all. She is one of those uncomplicated women like the mother in *Guest of Reality*. But Lagerkvist's main protagonists, *if* they can be seen as *one* portrait, depict complicated *and* divided personalities that suggest strongly alienated, suffering *man,* through the ages. Once again, as has been remarked, Lagerkvist has written an "evil tale," a variation of his common theme, "man and his peace of mind."

How did the loner Lagerkvist go about his work? And what did he think of inspiration? The simplicity of his style and themes is deceiving. It is obvious from early manuscripts of still unpublished works, placed at the Royal Library, Stockholm, after his death, that Lagerkvist tried many variations and made numerous changes in his writings, and that his longer works exacted great patience and effort before coming into being.

In his poetry and his novels, especially, complications and ambiguities abound: there are constant transpositions, developments, and juxtapositions of his previously used symbols. Sometimes his novels have to be read as more personal statements than might at first be apparent. A case in point is *The Sibyl,* which gives the appearance of a pagan myth but actually is Lagerkvist's *own* creation, and not a recreation of an already existing myth. And the main theme is almost exclusively on the realistic level, as we remember. The story turns on religious and existential questions but, as Gunnar Tideström has shown, it also deals with the poet's calling and the nature of the poet's inspiration.

When the novel opens, the old, furrowed pythia is sitting outside her house, watching it "with her old eyes . . . eyes that have seen god," and when it closes, she is looking out over the mighty landscape "with her old eyes." But she is really gazing inward, thinking of her youth, seeing the initiation of the new pythia. "But how long ago it is. . . ."

Three years before *Sibyllan*, Lagerkvist's *Aftonland* appeared. In it he wrote of a similar retrospective view, in almost the same words, only then he used the first person, suggesting the personal character of his theme:

> With old eyes I look back
> All is so long ago

In that collection the poet characterizes himself perhaps particularly in the lines:

> The god who does not exist,
> he it is who enkindles my soul,
> who makes my soul into a wilderness,
> a reeking ground, a scorched land, reeking after a fire.
> Because he does not exist.

The poet deliberately wrote "god" (i.e., lower case) in these later poems, while in his earlier verse he conventionally capitalized "God."

There are other indications that *The Sibyl* is a deeply personal work. The basic picture of his childhood years as well as the description of his early years with some changes can easily be read as a take-off on *Guest of Reality*. It is, therefore, tempting to speculate, with Tideström, about parallels between the sibyl's fate and that of the writer. When Lagerkvist decided that writing was his career, how did he determine it? Mustn't he have had some doubts? Was he *chosen* for such a task? What might his pious parents have thought, when their revolutionary, godless (!) son staked out the role of a prophet (!) for himself. If the sibyl was *chosen,* elected, to serve Apollo, how did *her* parents react?

Apollo is the god of prophecy, poetry, and music. He is also associated with Helios, the sun. Already on her first visit to the Apollo temple, the young pythia finds that she will not be tolerated in the upper halls of splendor and light of the temple, but rather in the lower regions, in the slimy pit. In her ecstasy and anxiety she is able to prophesy, put forth "dreadful, anguished sounds, utterly strange to me, and my lips moved without my will; it was not I who was doing this." Her inspired state requires interpreters, and a horde of others who make a living on her performance.

How does the pythia look upon these priests (interpreters) of the Apollo temple? She is utterly unimpressed by these "priests" (critics) and is sometimes quite glaringly scathing, as in the passage beginning with "Her inspiration was divine, no doubt, but it was they who interpreted it. . . ." And again: "She was possessed by god, certainly; god spoke through her. But it was they who knew what god really meant and wanted to say—they who knew how to penetrate the core of him and reveal it." Is it possible that Lagerkvist in those lines also had thrown in some doubts about the nature of his own calling?

If it is learned from inferences that the old lonely pythia has much in common with the novelist Lagerkvist, who also performed in "the lower regions," less effort is needed to spot a decisive similarity between Ahasuerus and Lagerkvist. Both of them had, in fact, declined to serve Jesus as their master: Ahasuerus by literally driving Jesus away from his house, and Anders (in *Guest of Reality*) by confessing that Jesus was "someone particularly repugnant to him." While Ahasuerus suffers from eternal unrest, a feeling of loneliness and meaninglessness (so familiar a theme in Lagerkvist's oeuvre), Lagerkvist himself from the very beginning became fixated to the idea of the *deus absconditus*, depicted as a preoccupied old woodcutter (in, for instance, *The Eternal Smile*) or a stone god with a scornful smile (in *The Holy Land*): "It was impassive, completely indifferent to man's entire world, disdainfully turned away from it, from everything."

Pär Lagerkvist more vigorously than any other professional writer explored religious concerns of both the modern heretic, influenced by modern science, and the modern brooder-searcher, an alienated outsider, desperately *wanting* to believe in traditional values. Persistently he came out as a nonbeliever, yet always with other possibilities open.

SELECTED BIBLIOGRAPHY

NOTE: *No attempt has been made here to list the numerous reviews, essays, articles, short stories, and poems by Lagerkvist. Indeed, only the major works of and about Lagerkvist are included. Especially useful are* Pär Lagerkvists Bibliografi / På Sextioårsdagen 23 maj 1951, *compiled by Uno Willers (Stockholm: Bonniers, 1951) and* Pär Lagerkvist in Translation: A Bibliography, *compiled by Anders Ryberg (Stockholm: Bonniers, 1964). Lagerkvist's Collected Works are to be found in: Skrifter 1–3, 1932; Dikter, 1941 and 1965; Prosa, 1945, 1956, and 1966; Dramatik, 1946 and 1956 (I–III). All those works were published by Bonniers, Stockholm.*

Principal Works of Pär Lagerkvist

(Unless otherwise stated, Bonniers, Stockholm, is the publisher)

"Gudstanken." Fantasi. Prosaskiss. Fram, 1912.
Människor. Stockholm: Frams förlag, 1912.
Ordkonst och bildkonst. Stockholm: Frams förlag, 1913.
Motiv. 1914.
Järn och människor. 1915.
Ångest. 1916.
Sista mänskan. 1917.
Teater. Den svåra stunden. 1918.
Kaos. 1919.
Det eviga leendet. 1920.
Den lyckliges väg. 1921.
Den osynlige. 1923.
Onda sagor. 1924.
Gäst hos verkligheten. 1925.
Hjärtats sånger. 1926.
Det besegrade livet. 1927.
Han som fick leva om sitt liv. 1928.
Kämpandeande. Bröllopsfesten, Guds lille handelsresande, Själarnas maskerad, Uppbrottet. 1930.

Vid lägereld. 1932.
Konungen. 1932.
Bödeln. 1933.
Den knutna näven. 1934.
I den tiden. 1935.
Mannen utan själ. 1936.
Genius. 1937.
Den befriade människan. 1939.
Seger i mörker. 1939.
Sång och strid. 1940.
Midsommardröm i fattighuset. 1941.
Hemmet och stjärnan. 1942.
Dvärgen. 1944.
De vises sten. 1947.
Låt människan leva. 1949.
Barabbas. 1950.
Aftonland. 1953.
Sibyllan. 1956.
Ahasverus död. 1960.
Pilgrim på havet. 1962.
Det heliga landet. 1964.
Mariamne. 1967.

Selected Translations of Lagerkvist's Works

The Dwarf. Translated by Alexandra Dick. New York: Hill and Wang, 1945.

Twentieth-Century Scandinavian Poetry. Ed. by Martin S. Allwood. Stockholm: K F, 1950.

Barabbas. Translated by Alan Blair. New York: Random House, 1951.

Let Man Live. Translated by Henry Alexander and Llewellyn Jones. In *Scandinavian Plays of the Twentieth Century*. Third Series. Princeton, N.J.: Princeton University Press, 1951.

Midsummer Dream in the Workhouse. Translated by Alan Blair. London: W. Hodge, 1953.

The Eternal Smile and Other Stories. Translated by Alan Blair, Erik Mesterton, Denys W. Harding, Carl Eric Lindin. New York: Random House, 1954. Introduction by Richard B. Vowles.

The Sibyl. Translated by Naomi Walford. New York: Random House, 1960.

Seven Swedish Poets. Translated by Frederic Fleisher. Malmö and Staffanstorp: Bo Cavefors, 1963.

Pilgrim at Sea. Translated by Naomi Walford. New York: Random House, 1964.

The Holy Land. Translated by Naomi Walford. New York: Random House, 1966.

Pär Lagerkvist: Modern Theatre: Seven Plays and an Essay. Translated by Thomas Buckman. Lincoln: University of Nebraska Press, 1966.

Herod and Mariamne. Translated by Naomi Walford. New York: Knopf, 1968.

The Man Who Lived His Life Over. Translated by Walter Gustafsson. In *Five Modern Scandinavian Plays*. New York: Twayne, 1971.

The Eternal Smile: Three Stories. Translated by Erik Mesterton, Denys W. Harding, David O'Gorman, New York: Hill & Wang, 1971.

Evening Land. Translated by W. H. Auden and Leif Sjöberg. Detroit: Wayne State University Press, 1975.

Critical Works and Commentary

Abenius, M. "Mörkret som symbol i Barabbas," *BLM*, 20 (1951), No. 4, 285–87.

Ahlenius, H. "Barabbas, vår like," *BLM*, 19 (1950).

Åslund, L. "Pär Lagerkvists *Ordkonst och bildkonst* och det nya måleriet," *Ord och Bild*, 64 (1955), 35–49.

Beijer, Agne. "Two Swedish Dramatists, Pär Lagerkvist and Hjalmar Bergman," *World Theatre*, 4 (1955), 14–24.

Benson, A. B. "Pär Lagerkvist: Nobel Laureate," *College English*, 13 (May 1952), 417–24.

Bergman, Gösta M. Pär Lagerkvists dramatik. Stockholm: Norstedt, 1928.

Blomberg, Erik. "Det besegrade livet: en studie i Pär Lagerkvists författarskap," Ord och Bild, 42, (1933), 201–14, 267–78, 325–32.

Brandell, Gunnar. Svensk litteratur 1900–1950. Stockholm: Örnkrona, 1958; Stockholm: Aldus, 1965. Revised and extended with Jan Stenkvist as Svensk litteratur: 1870–1970. Stockholm: Aldus, 1974–75.

Braybrooke, N. "Pär Lagerkvist," Catholic World, 176 (January 1953), 266.

Brunius, Teddy. "Det kubistiska experimentet," BLM, 23 (1954), 805–14.

Buckman, Ths. "Pär Lagerkvist and the Swedish Theatre," Tulane Drama Review, 6 (1961), 3–89.

——. "Stylistic and Textual Changes in Modern Teater," Scandinavian Studies, 33 (August 1961), 137–49.

Ellestad, Everett M. "Pär Lagerkvist and Cubism: A Study of His Theory and Practice," Scandinavian Studies, 45 (Winter 1973), 37–52.

Fearnley, Ragnhild. Pär Lagerkvist. Oslo: Gyldendal, 1950.

Fredén, Gustaf. Pär Lagerkvist: Från Gudstanken till Barabbas. Stockholm: Bonniers, 1952 and 1954.

Granlid, H.O. Det medvetna barnet. Stil och innebörd i Pär Lagerkvists Gäst hos verkligheten. Göteborg: Gumperts, 1961.

Gustafson, Alrik. A History of Swedish Literature. Minneapolis: University of Minnesota Press, 1961.

Hallberg, Peter. "Stjärnsymboliken i Pär Lagerkvists lyrik," Göteborgs-studier i litteraturhistoria tillägnade Sverker Ek (1954), 313–42.

Heggelund, Kjell. Fiksjon og virkelighet. Oslo: Scandinavian University Books, 1966, pp. 11–41.

Henmark, Kai. Fågel av eld: Essäer om dikt och engagemang. Stockholm: Bonniers, 1962.

——. Främlingen Lagerkvist. Stockholm: Tema; Rabén & Sjögren, 1966.

Hörnström, Erik. Pär Lagerkvist: Från Den röda tiden till det Eviga leendet. Stockholm: Bonniers, 1947.

Johannesson, Eric O. "Pär Lagerkvist and the Art of Rebellion," Scandinavian Studies, 30 (February 1958), 19–29.

Lagerroth, Erland. Svensk Berättarkonst. Lund: Gleerup, 1968.

Larsson, Bengt. "Pär Lagerkvists litterära kubism," Samlaren, 85 (1965), 66–95.

Linder, Erik Hjalmar. Fem decennier av nitton-hundratalet. Stockholm: Natur och Kultur, 1966.

Linnér, Sven. "Pär Lagerkvists barndomsmiljö," *Samlaren,* 58 (1947), 53–90.

——. Livsförsoning och idyll: En studie i rikssvensk litteratur 1915– 1925. Uppsala: 1954 (dissertation).

——. "Pär Lagerkvist's 'The Eternal Smile' and 'The Sibyl,'" *Scandinavian Studies,* 37 (May 1965), 160–67.

——. Pär Lagerkvists livstro. Stockholm: Bonniers, 1961.

Linnér, Sven, ed. "Special Issue Devoted to the Work of Pär Lagerkvist," *Scandinavica,* 10 (May 1971).

Malmström, Gunnel. Menneskehjertets verden: Hovedmotiv i Pär Lagerkvists diktning. Oslo: Gyldendal, 1970.

Mjöberg, Jöran. "Det förnekade mörkret," *Samlaren* 35 (1954), 78– 112.

——. Livsproblemet hos Lagerkvist. Stockholm: Bonniers, 1951.

Oberholzer, Otto. Pär Lagerkvist: Studien zu seiner Prosa und seiner Dramen. Heidelberg: Carl Winter, 1958.

Scobbie, Irene. "Contrasting Characters in *Barabbas,*" *Scandinavian Studies,* 32 (November 1960), 212–20.

——. Pär Lagerkvist: An Introduction. Stockholm: The Swedish Institute, 1963.

Skartveit, Andreas. Gud skapt i menneskets bilete: Ein Lagerkviststudie. Oslo: Det Norske Samlaget, 1966.

Spector, Robert Donald. "Lagerkvist and Existentialism," *Scandinavian Studies,* 32 (November 1960), 203–11.

——. "Lagerkvist's Uses of Deformity," *Scandinavian Studies,* 33 (November 1961), 209–17.

——. Pär Lagerkvist. New York: Twayne (World Authors Series), 1973.

Stenström, Thure. Berättartekniska studier i Pär Lagerkvists, Lars Gyllenstens och Cora Sandels prosa. Stockholm: Svenska Bokförlaget, 1964.

Swanson, Roy A. "Evil and Love in Lagerkvist's Crucifixion Cycle," *Scandinavian Studies,* 38 (November 1966), 302–17.

Tideström, Gunnar. "Tankar kring Pär Lagerkvists *Sibyllan,*" *Samlaren,* 80 (1959), 80–96.

Tideström, Gunnar, ed. Synpunkter på Pär Lagerkvist. Stockholm: Bonniers, 1966.

Vowles, Richard B. "The Fiction of Pär Lagerkvist," *Western Humanities Review,* 8 (1954), 111–19.

Weathers, Winston. Pär Lagerkvist: A Critical Essay. Grand Rapids, Mich.: William B. Eerdmans, 1968.

Werin, Algot. "Det onda är odödligt . . ." *Svenskt 1800-tal* (1948).

Wigforss, Brita. "Pär Lagerkvist och Dostojevski," *Ord och Bild,* 70 (1961), 169–77.